STUDIES IN FRENCH LITERATURE No. 15

General Editor
W. G. Moore
Fellow and Tutor of St. John's College, Oxford

MOLIÈRE:
LES PRÉCIEUSES
RIDICULES

by
BRONNIE TRELOAR

EDWARD ARNOLD

First published 1970 by
Edward Arnold (Publishers) Ltd.,
41 Maddox Street, London W.1.

Cloth edition SBN: 7131 5496 9

Paper edition SBN: 7131 5500 0

Printed in Great Britain by
The Camelot Press Ltd., London and Southampton

Contents

Introduction

It is certainly a mistake to approach *Les Précieuses ridicules* in a respectful manner, as a piece of literature written by one of the great figures of the *Grand Siècle*. Think of it rather as a short, topical, satirical entertainment, designed to round off an evening of more serious fare, and enjoy it for its pace and dash and rollicking fun. Its author would have made an admirable script-writer for television. Above all, as Molière makes clear in his preface, it should be seen and acted rather than read.

We will come much nearer to understanding the play and catching its spirit by taking it at its face value and enjoying its gusto than by treating it as a blow in a battle between two warring factions (though an eminent scholar has seen it as this) or by debating too earnestly its value as a piece of social comment. First and foremost, the play was written to entertain, to 'get the audience in'. We will do better to join the mob in the pit and let Molière entertain us as well, than to stand at the door of the theatre arguing too long about the play's implications. Molière himself, one feels, would have been the first to make fun of anyone so foolish as to write ponderously about his delicious trifle. The critic runs the risk of becoming a latter-day Mascarille, weightily underlining the obvious: 'Avez-vous remarqué ce commencement? Oh! oh! Voilà qui est extraordinaire! oh! oh! Comme un homme qui s'avise tout d'un coup: oh! oh! La surprise: oh! oh!'

On the other hand, a certain amount of background information is, if not strictly necessary, at least desirable, if only to give some sort of three-dimensional quality to the play and to make good a little of what we have lost, in the way of everyday common knowledge, in the intervening three hundred years. The object of part of this study, then, will be to re-create its context round the play and to try to restore to it some of the impact which it must have had when it was first presented.

If you had been to see the first performance of *Les Précieuses ridicules* in November 1659 at the Petit-Bourbon, it would have been in nothing like the frame of mind in which you might go to the Comédie-Française today to see a distinguished company perform a Molière play. To understand the impression it made when it was first performed, you must think yourself back to the seventeenth century. You must be there, in the theatre, and see it for the first time.

You are probably one of the upper bourgeoisie in Paris. You go to the theatre a good deal; it is one of the favourite recreations of the circle in which you move. If you belong to the *hoi polloi* of course you probably go to watch the free shows, the quacks and mountebanks on the Pont Neuf, or if there is a public hanging you might rather go to watch that. Let us assume, however, that you belong to the theatre-going public. There are several theatres which you attend. Most often you go to the Hôtel de Bourgogne. The company there does tragedy splendidly, in the stately and stylised way to which you are accustomed. They roll out their lines in a way which we should probably call 'ham' today. You might go to the Marais, or perhaps you will go to see the Italians playing at the Petit-Bourbon. They play in Italian, but a good deal of it is mime, and they are marvellous comics.

Then you remember that they only play on certain days, and on the others, the less popular days, a new company plays there, the Troupe de Monsieur. That actor Molière runs it. Tonight he is doing *Cinna*, and you have heard that he is not very good in tragedy, but there is something else billed for the same performance, a farce called *Les Précieuses ridicules*, by Molière himself. Though he is not yet very well known as an author, he has already put on two successful plays of his own in Paris, comedies of intrigue in the Italian manner. The title of this new offering sounds promising. Everyone is talking about the *précieuses* these days, and the adjective *ridicules* gives you the clue you need. You like a good farce, and this is a new one. So you decide to go.

Imagine the scene inside the theatre. The pit is full of standing people, jostling, craning, moving about, with a certain amount of scuffling near the doors as lackeys and other non-paying would-be spectators are ejected. The quality sits in the gallery which runs round three sides of the theatre, and a number of young bloods are actually seated on the stage. They are there as much to be seen as to see. There is probably a high degree of audience participation.

The evening proceeds, and at last *Cinna* is over. The actors have made a quick change. Molière has got into his elaborate and absurd *marquis* costume. Probably the audience is restless by now, but most of it is staying for the new farce. The need to make a quick impact is obvious.

The play is in prose, in itself a change from the noble alexandrines of *Cinna*. A few brief exchanges between La Grange and Du Croisy tell us enough of the situation to intrigue us, and then in comes Gorgibus, the typical comic father-figure of farce, perennially popular. By this time the audience knows what to expect, or thinks it does, but there are surprises in store. Immediately after Gorgibus come Magdelon and Cathos, and they are not quite like anything the Parisian public has seen before. Then, while the audience is still laughing over their high-flown language, in comes Molière as Mascarille, in his fantastic costume, with all his comic art at his finger tips, and from that moment the success of the evening is assured.

This first performance, so successful that the admission price was doubled thereafter, marked the beginning of Molière's brilliant career in Paris. Though not his first play it was the first which bore the unmistakable stamp of his own particular brand of comedy, and it became the talk of the town.

Nine months later François Donneau wrote:

> L'on est venu à Paris de vingt lieues à la ronde afin d'en avoir le divertissement; il n'était fils de bonne mère, qui, lorsque l'on la jouait, ne s'empressât pour la voir des premiers, et ceux qui font profession de galanterie et qui n'avaient pas vu représenter les *Précieuses* d'abord qu'elles commencèrent à faire parler d'elles, n'osaient l'avouer sans rougir.[1]

Donneau goes on to say that a few of Molière's rivals were grudging in their praises of the play. Some said that its success was due to the acting rather than to the play itself. Others said that the fact that everyone was interested in the *précieuses* at that time was the cause of its popularity, and that the author would certainly find it difficult to repeat his success.

How wrong they were proved in the event! With *Les Précieuses ridicules*, Molière had arrived.

[1] François Donneau, Preface to his comedy *La Cocue imaginaire*, 14 August 1660.

I

What is Preciosity?

Since the subject was a topical one in 1659, we should look briefly at preciosity and the *précieuses*, trying to see them through the eyes of a man of their time.

A distinction must be made between present-day and seventeenth-century use of terms. Today the word preciosity is applied to two things. First, it is used to describe a particular style of writing, consciously clever, its charm deriving chiefly from the wit of its conceits and from the nonchalant and graceful mastery of technical difficulties. It was valued principally as an exercise in these drawing-room qualities. Secondly, it is applied to a social phenomenon characterised by the emergence of women as arbiters of taste in the literary *salons*.

The seventeenth century did not use the word preciosity with the first or precisely with the second of these meanings. What we know as the precious style in literature was simply the *style galant*. The social pheno-menon had no name. It flourished, it fascinated contemporary observers, including Molière, but it was not labelled.

The use of the word *précieux* too, in the sense of a precious poet or exponent of the *style galant*, is chiefly though not exclusively a modern one. Its feminine form, on the other hand, had a great vogue in the seventeenth century, and was used then as now to describe the ladies who reigned in the literary *salons*. It had, however, some overtones which it has lost today. Its flavour was often slightly derogatory, or at least tinged with amusement, as if one were to speak, with a smile, of the 'New Woman'. It was rarely, until Somaize's *Grand Dictionnaire* of 1661, attached to a particular person. We may think of Mme de Rambouillet as the first of the great *précieuses*, but it would not have occurred to her contemporaries so to call her. To them she was simply Mme de Rambouillet, a person, not a type.

From the sixteen-fifties onwards, more women than ever before began to discover that by organising literary gatherings and cultivating the art of conversation, and by using whatever intelligence, wit and judgment they were endowed with, they could make an interesting life for themselves within the framework of the existing social conventions. Pioneers in their day, they were subjected to a certain amount of raillery and given the not wholly flattering name of *précieuses*. While the movement itself was outstandingly successful, the name tended to provoke a smile. It is significant that no one ever described herself as a *précieuse*, or wished to be called one. 'Leur humilité les a même fait déclarer ennemies de tous ceux qui les appellent du nom de précieuse, que leur esprit seul leur a fait donner,' says Somaize in his half-mocking manner, and Sorel adds: 'On a parlé des précieuses comme si c'était quelque nouvel ordre de femmes et de filles qui fissent plus les capables que les autres en leurs discours et en leurs manières d'agir; mais nous n'en avons jamais vu aucune qui ait voulu avouer d'en être.'[1]

The distinction between true and false *précieuses*, arbitrarily made in the seventeenth century to avoid giving offence and perpetuated ever since, is misleading. No one was anxious to be called a true *précieuse* either. All that may safely be said is that in this field as in all others, there were those who had flair and those who lacked it. Women whose names are still known to us today, like Mme de Sablé, Mme de la Suze and a host of others, succeeded in running famous *salons* because they had wit, charm, intelligence and personal magnetism. Inevitably there were also those who, lacking these qualities, produced dreary copies of the real thing.

It seems that at first people were very curious about the *précieuses*, and a little uncertain. The word tended to be used in an abstract way, like *coquette*, to describe a type. The seventeenth century had a passion for dividing women into labelled categories, *précieuses*, *prudes*, *bigotes*, *savantes*, *pédantes*, *coquettes*, *galantes* and so on. (You will remember La Grange's remark in Scene i: 'En un mot, c'est un ambigu de précieuse et de coquette que leur personne.') There was nothing fixed about any of these categories. If an author happened to be writing about the *précieuses*, he might make the other classes subdivisions of the *genus précieuse*, as does the abbé de Pure. The author of *La Déroute des Précieuses* equates the *précieuses* with the *prudes*, since his *ballet-mascarade* was designed to please and amuse the rather licentious court of Gaston

[1] *De la Connaissance des bons Livres*, 1671, p. 370.

d'Orléans. Somaize on the other hand, self-constituted champion of the *précieuses* when it suited him, remarks:

> Qu'on ne me vienne donc pas conter toutes ces chimères: que les précieuses sont des filles qui ne se veulent point marier, qu'il faut qu'elles soient âgées de quarante-cinq ans, qu'elles soient laides, et cent autres choses de cette nature, que l'erreur du vulgaire a produites avec aussi peu de raison que de fondement.[2]

If then we have to accept the fact that the terminology was confused, we may ask what was the reality behind the confusion, and behind the bantering tone which was sometimes kindly but sometimes the reverse. What qualities and activities made a woman a *précieuse*?

The word itself came into general currency about 1654, though there are isolated examples of its use much earlier. In that year the chevalier de Sévigné included as a news-item in a letter: 'Il y a une nature de filles et de femmes à Paris que l'on nomme Précieuses', and already he accused them of affectation, a charge often levelled in the next few years.

There are a great number of other references to them, but the most detailed information we have about them is contained in *La Prétieuse ou le Mystère des Ruelles* (1656-58). Its author, the abbé Michel de Pure, wealthy and of good family, haunted the *ruelles* and recorded many of the conversations he heard there. Even allowing for the fact that his book is a work of fiction, a loosely-knit *roman à clef*, and that the conversations are written by himself and not recorded verbatim, they still have an air of authenticity. De Pure's *précieuses* talk about language and about literature; they discuss love and friendship, subtly analysing fine shades of emotion; and they talk about the position of women in society, especially the question of arranged marriages in which the woman's wishes are not consulted. De Pure was impressed, not to say surprised, to find that women could hold their own with men in a discussion. 'Elles ont la réponse aussi vive, le jugement aussi solide, le discernement aussi exact que l'homme les peut avoir,' he says, and goes on to add that they have a charming and polished way of expressing their thoughts.[3] Nowhere do we find his *précieuses* indulging in the vapid conversation or ridiculous jargon of a Magdelon or a Cathos. De Pure

[2] *Grand Dictionnaire des Précieuses*, edited by Livet, Vol. I, p. 23.
[3] *La Prétieuse*, edited by Magne, Vol. I, pp. 165-6.

was none the less a man of his century, and although his picture of the *précieuses* is on the whole favourable to them, the bantering tone creeps in. Half-admiring, he is still a little uncertain of what attitude he should adopt.

Antoine Baudeau de Somaize in his *Grand Dictionnaire des Précieuses* of 1661 takes this same equivocal attitude. Somaize was a literary hack of no great distinction, bent upon exploiting Molière's success with *Les Précieuses ridicules*, so that his testimony is rather suspect; but there is something to be learned from his pages. He sums up the qualities which were considered characteristic of a *précieuse*:

> Les loix des précieuses consistent en l'observance exacte des modes, en l'attache indispensable de la nouveauté, en la nécessité d'avoir un alcôviste particulier, ou du moins d'en recevoir plusieurs; en celle de tenir ruelle, ce qui peut passer pour la principale: car, pour être pré-cieuse, il faut ou tenir assemblée chez soi, ou aller chez celles qui en tiennent. C'est encore une loi assez reçue parmi elles de lire toutes les nouveautés, et surtout les romans, de savoir faire des vers et des billets doux. . . . Je suis certain que la première partie d'une précieuse est l'esprit, et que pour porter ce nom il est absolument nécessaire qu'une personne en ait.[4]

This quizzical tone which both de Pure and Somaize adopt in speaking of the *précieuses* probably represented the attitude of most men of the seventeenth century towards them—indulgent, a little surprised that women should begin to invade their province, half-amused, half-admiring, their praises always tempered by irony. Perhaps it would be truer to say that this was the attitude towards the abstract idea of the *précieuse*. In fact the *salons* or *ruelles* run by the most successful women were immensely popular. Poets and writers of the day thronged them; the gallant and worldly *abbés* shone there; between campaigns, martial dukes bandied epigrams with aristocratic ladies; anthologies of precious poetry and prose were compiled; fashions in literary games came and went; arguments over the rival merits of two sonnets provoked spates of clever verse extolling one or the other.

It is perhaps difficult for us today to appreciate the pleasure which the *précieuses* and their friends found in the creation of these

[4] *Op. cit. Loix, Antiquité.*

fragile literary trifles, and in the versified repartee at which they excelled. The gaiety and verbal brilliance of their gatherings are lost to us. Like the actor's art, they are ephemeral. From the *Chroniques du Samedi*, from Conrart's manuscripts, from the *Recueil La Suze-Pellisson* and other collections we can catch a little of the charm and gaiety of the *salon* or *ruelle*, but we must be prepared to make a leap of the imagination to re-create the atmosphere in which these trifles were born.

One may well ask, where does Molière's comedy stand in relation to all this? It is apparent, as a matter of historical fact, that it did nothing to alter the course of preciosity, since the *salons* continued to flourish and precious literature to be written and enjoyed long after the publication of *Les Précieuses ridicules*. Nor was there any reason why it should affect this prevailing trend. The comedy is based on the fact that two silly girls, newly arrived in Paris with their eyes fixed on the glittering world of the *salons*, ingenuously attempt to pass themselves off as members of it, and in so doing become victims of a more clever deception.

In the year 1659, as we have seen, the word *précieuse*, and even more the idea, provoked a smile. Everyone wanted to hear about these odd creatures; no one thought of herself as a *précieuse*. An abstract conception, however, is useless as a subject for comedy. Molière makes his comic heroines into real people. Magdelon and Cathos are flesh and blood *petites bourgeoises* from the provinces. They are no less real because he draws them for the stage in the big bold strokes of caricature. His need when he wrote *Les Précieuses ridicules* was to amuse his audience and to provide them with an entertainment which they would not find at the rival Hôtel de Bourgogne or elsewhere. He disdained nothing which would make them laugh, and people have been laughing ever since at his two sillies aping the manners of a world of which they have only the foggiest conception.

II

The Comedy

i Place

We have seen that in writing *Les Précieuses ridicules* Molière was motivated by an urgent need for success at the end of this, the first year in which his newly-named *Troupe de Monsieur* was playing to Parisian audiences.

The citizens of the capital had an insatiable appetite for novelty, nowhere more apparent than among the leisured members of the upper bourgeoisie and aristocracy who formed the most constant element of the theatre-going public. The first thing Molière had done, on establishing his company in the capital, was to offer his audience 'pour nouveautés' two comedies of his own, *L'Étourdi* and *Le Dépit amoureux*, which were new to Parisian audiences, although they had been played in the provinces. La Grange, to whose Register we owe this information, makes the point that each of these comedies 'passa pour nouvelle à Paris' and notes that 'ces deux pièces nouvelles ou telles ne contribuèrent pas peu au succès de la Troupe.'

After twelve months in the capital, Molière may well have felt the need to woo his public with another novelty. This time it was to be a sprightly entertainment with topical interest, but firmly based upon a tried and tested formula. This judicious blend of elements which were familiar and popular with others which were novel and topical was to prove a highly successful experiment.

We may look first at the traditional elements on which the play is based. Molière was working within the framework of farce, and he did not hesitate to use its buffoonery and horse-play to provide his comedy with movement and action. The sight of an irascible old man, stick in hand, beating the unpaid musicians off the stage was very much to the taste of a seventeenth-century audience.

When Jodelet comes on the scene, he introduces the *lazzi* which were an important part of the *commedia dell'arte*. These comic gestures, of which there are some indications in the text, may well have been much more extensive in the stage version, and perhaps depended a good deal on Jodelet himself, who doubtless gauged his audience's reactions and played accordingly. It appears too from Mlle Desjardins' account of the first performance, which she calls, significantly, '*La Farce* des Précieuses', that the stage version contained other earthy gestures, such as the use of what the ladies euphemistically refer to as a 'soucoupe inférieure'.

Italian comedians—and Molière had trained under the greatest of these—based their art on improvisation and mime. It would not be surprising if much of this found its way into Molière's production of *Les Précieuses ridicules*. It is an actor's play, written for actors, and it is probably fair to assume that not everything which was played on the stage appears in the published version. In his preface, he affects surprise at finding himself for the first time in print, in the company of 'Messieurs les auteurs', thus clearly underlining the fact that at this period he thought of himself primarily as an actor, to whom authors were another species. He stresses, too, his play's connections with farce by his remark that since the antics of the Doctor and the Captain—both characters of the *commedia dell'arte*—do not offend real scholars and men of action, neither should the *précieuses* be offended by his caricature of their imitators.

For three of his characters, Molière draws on the stock figures of farce, the old man, the cunning servant, and the braggart soldier, types which had retained their popularity down the centuries from Latin comedy, through the *commedia dell'arte*, to French farce. To these stock types, however, he adds a new dimension. Social satire and the contemporary scene begin to appear on the stage. Gorgibus is not just the silly old pantaloon of farce; he is an immediately recognisable type, the thrifty, hard-headed *bon bourgeois de province*. Mascarille is much more than a rascally, clever valet. He has become a new contemporary type, the Parisian fop and literary man-about-town.

Les Précieuses ridicules had a forerunner, some twenty years before, in Desmarets' *Les Visionnaires* (1637) in which Mélisse, like Magdelon and Cathos, is so carried away by the reading of history and novels that she has lost touch with reality, while Hespérie, who thinks all men are in love with her, is an ancestor of Bélise in *Les Femmes savantes*. The pretensions and silliness of women offered a rich comic vein which had already been tapped, and was now waiting for Molière to exploit more fully. Since he had acted in Desmarets' play in the very year in which he produced *Les Précieuses ridicules*, the comic possibilities of feminine folly were likely to be uppermost in his mind.

Further promptings in this direction, if such were needed, may have come from recollections of Lyons, where Molière had spent much time on his provincial tours. There, in 1656, Chappuzeau had published *Le Cercle des Femmes*, which depicts a *salon* of militant feminists. It is at least possible that Molière remembered the comedy value of such a subject when he was shaping *Les Précieuses ridicules*. Even the plot is similar. A rejected suitor seeks to humiliate his erstwhile lady-love by sending a young peasant disguised as a nobleman to visit her.

Finally, the idea for the plot was probably confirmed by another play produced by Molière only three months before the first performance of *Les Précieuses ridicules*. This was Scarron's *L'Héritier ridicule* which hinges on a like deception. A suitor sends his valet to his lady in the guise of his cousin, said to be the new heir to the family fortune. This kind of title, too, was a common one. The adjective *ridicule* features in the names of at least seven farces and light comedies published between 1655 and 1664.

It is not only the plot and the title which contain echoes of Scarron's play. Molière also incorporated into *Les Précieuses ridicules* a joke which had apparently been very successful in the Scarron production, the enumeration of odd cosmetics. Molière's list of 'blancs d'œuf, lait virginal, lard, pieds de mouton' is very close to Scarron's 'coques d'œuf, lard et pieds de mouton . . . lait virginal'.

Even the idea of writing a comedy about the *précieuses* is not, surprisingly, Molière's own invention. Three contemporary writers claim that Molière based his comedy on a play by the abbé de Pure written in Italian and acted in 1656 by the Italian troupe in Paris. Somaize, in the preface to his comedy *Les Véritables Précieuses* (January 1660) writes: 'Il (Molière) a copié *les Précieuses* de M. l'abbé de Pure jouée par les Italiens', and in Scene vii of the same play he claims that the plot was similar: 'C'est la même chose, ce sont deux valets . . . qui se déguisent pour plaire à deux femmes et que leurs maîtres battent à la fin.' The rhymed bulletin *La Muse royale* for 3 May 1660 also mentions de Pure's play:

> ... *Les Précieuses*
> *Ridicules, cela s'entend,*
> *Qu'un génie assez éclatant*
> *Savoir le sieur abbé de Pure*
> *En langue toscane fort pure*
> *Fit dans Bourbon parler jadis* ...

Lastly, Donneau de Visé in his *Nouvelles nouvelles* of 1663 writes of Molière:

> Comme il n'était encore ni assez hardi pour entreprendre une satire, ni assez capable pour en venir à bout, il eut recours aux Italiens, ses bons amis, et accommoda les *Précieuses* au théâtre français, qui avaient été jouées sur le leur et qui leur avaient été données par un abbé des plus galants.

Somaize and Donneau de Visé were of course no friends to Molière, and this cry of plagiarism was a favourite accusation of the lesser fry on the literary scene, reflecting no doubt the importance of novelty already mentioned. The authorship of any new idea with popular appeal tended to be disputed.

How much Molière's comedy may have owed to de Pure's play on the same subject cannot be determined, since de Pure's work has not survived. Most probably it owed very little, for Molière was not in Paris in 1656 when it was performed, and as there is no record of its publication, it is unlikely that he read it. De Pure's play seems to have made little impact on the theatre-going public, and the fact that it was in Italian must have severely limited its popular appeal.

It is apparent, however, that Molière, though he was the first to exploit fully the comic possibilities of the subject, was not the first with the idea of a comedy about the *précieuses*.

While there is much that is new in *Les Précieuses ridicules*, it will be seen that there is also much that was part of the stock-in-trade of the theatre. It has its place mid-way between farce and comedy of manners. Backward-looking to traditional ingredients that had long delighted French audiences, it also points forward to the new style of comedy which Molière was to make his own. While it can claim little originality in the matter of plot, and was not even the first play about the *précieuses*, it is distinguished from its predecessors by its rich comic invention and eminent actability.

More important than this perhaps is the fact that here, for the first time, Molière was putting contemporary types on the stage with a verve and deftness of touch which brought immediate recognition.

The court and *salon* atmosphere in Paris had produced a high degree of sophistication and with it came a more developed taste for social satire. Molière recognised and supplied this need. After commenting on 'the fact that he borrowed the idea for his *Précieuses* from de Pure, Donneau de Visé goes on to remark: 'Il les habilla admirablement bien à la française, et la réussite qu'elles eurent lui fit connaître que l'on aimait la satire et la bagatelle. Il connut par là les goûts du siècle.'

Mascarille, Magdelon and Cathos are among the first in Molière's long gallery of portraits and caricatures of people whom his contemporaries saw about them every day. Blue-stockings, poetasters, fops, quacks, bores, unctuous parasites, *nouveaux riches* and the provincial gentry, they are all there. Even the hard-pressed actor-producer, rushing to fulfil a royal command for entertainment at short notice, is among them: Molière put himself on the stage as he put the rest of society. A man of the theatre, he saw things in terms of the theatre, and his stage is filled with people drawn from life, just a little larger than life-size.

ii People

The principal characters in *Les Précieuses ridicules* fall into pairs: La Grange and Du Croisy, the two suitors; then Gorgibus and Marotte, plain blunt people both; then our pair of heroines, Magdelon and Cathos; and finally Mascarille and Jodelet, the two valets disguised as a *marquis* and a *vicomte* respectively. This last quartet consists of a pair of fools and a pair of knaves, and it is from the encounter between knave and fool that the comedy springs.

Of the suitors there is little to say. They make their brief appearance at the beginning and end of the play simply to open the action and to tie up the plot; unlike the comic characters, they have no particular personality of their own. Their names are their real ones. La Grange and Du Croisy were both newcomers to Molière's company at this time, and La Grange, then twenty years old, was being trained for the *jeune premier* parts which he took in most of the later plays.

It is to this same actor that posterity owes a great debt for much of the information we have about Molière and his company. He kept the Register, in which he faithfully noted down details of performances, attendances, box-office receipts and so on, as well as some of the major events in the personal lives of the company. After Molière's death, he took over its management.

Of the next pair, the maid-servant Marotte barely rates a mention. She is simply a brief sketch for all the later servants in Molière, who are usually forthright in speech, very much a part of the family, and full of good down-to-earth common sense. She is destined to reappear in *Les Femmes savantes* as Martine, also baffled by the exalted language of her mistresses. Marotte is a comic form of the name Marie, and the part was played by Marie Ragueneau de l'Estang, who later married La Grange.

Gorgibus, the archetypal comic father figure, has a more substantial rôle. The name and the character were already familiar to the public. Gorgibus appears in farces by other authors, and Molière himself had put him on the stage twice before, in the farces *La Jalousie du Barbouillé* and *Le Médecin volant*. He uses the name again in his next play, *Le Cocu imaginaire*.

The Gorgibus of *Les Précieuses ridicules* is a strongly drawn character. He could be counted on to get the play away to a good start. With practically his first words he reveals a situation which was no doubt as familiar in Molière's day as in ours, the clash of generations. Magdelon and Cathos have been spending far too much money on beauty preparations. When the play opens, the girls are upstairs making yet another lip-salve. For Gorgibus, it is a matter of ridiculous expenditure on 'greasing their snouts', and this forthright remark serves as an excellent foil for Magdelon's high-flown opening words.

We know from Mlle Desjardins' account that Gorgibus spoke pompously 'd'un air d'orateur breton', and that his clothes were old-fashioned, thereby further underlining the provincial origins of the trio. His rather rigid and conventional cast of mind is suggested in a few speeches. He is fond of preaching ('Je te dis que le mariage est une chose sainte et sacrée'), of stereotyped expressions and pieces of homespun wisdom.

He has brought his daughter and niece to the capital to get them married. No doubt the trip has already cost him a good deal of money and will cost him more before the question of the dowry is settled. As if this were not enough, the girls are now squandering money like water. Relief is in sight, however. He has found two highly suitable prospective husbands, and they have just come to present their respects to the girls. It is at this point in the tide of his affairs that things begin to go wrong. The suitors are observed departing very dissatisfied. Gorgibus calls the girls down and learns of the total sabotage of his plans. Cathos and Magdelon, carried away by their romantic reading, want their wooing to run the full course of the romances described in one of Madeleine de Scudéry's novels, all ten volumes of it.

Thus we are made aware at once of the divergence between parental plans for them and their own intentions, with the growing contrast between Gorgibus, feet firmly planted on the ground, more and more bewildered by the incomprehensible behaviour of his daughter and niece, and the girls, heads in the clouds, sailing every minute further out of touch with reality. In the end Gorgibus storms out, thinking he has had the last word: 'Either you both get married straight away, or into the convent you go!' In fact, as we see, it is the girls who have the last word, behind his back, in one final flight of romantic day-dreaming. They feel convinced that they cannot really be related to anyone so pedestrian as Gorgibus. Perhaps, some day, some romantic secret may be revealed to show that they are more nobly born. . . .

These two short scenes serve to show us that the two girls are very far from being *précieuses*, in spite of the high-flown language which they try out on Gorgibus. What emerges clearly is that they are young, naïve and romantic, a pair of ninnies with social aspirations. The real *précieuses*, of whom we know a great deal, were almost all married women of good social standing, or else they were women of exceptional calibre and mistresses of households, like Madeleine de Scudéry.

Magdelon and Cathos are virtually two halves of the same character; there is very little that distinguishes one from the other. Magdelon perhaps more often takes the lead. Cathos tends to be her echo. Their names come from the Christian names of the two actresses who played the parts. Cathos[1] was Catherine de Brie, wife of another of the actors, and Magdelon was that old trouper Madeleine Béjart. At the time of the first production of *Les Précieuses ridicules* she would have been in her early forties, but no doubt, like many another actress, perfectly capable of playing a young girl. For Magdelon and Cathos *were* green young girls, straight from the country. In this respect the title of the play is misleading. One tends to think 'this is a play about the *précieuses*, who were ridiculous'. In fact it is in their attempts to pass themselves off as something which they are not that the heroines are ridiculous. In the same way, the title of Scarron's *Héritier ridicule* refers not to a ridiculous heir, but to one whose pretensions to being the heir are ridiculous.

It is because the girls are so unsophisticated and gullible that they fall easy victims to Mascarille when he offers them *entrée* to the world they long to enter. He seems to them the very personification of the aristocratic literary gentleman, but you and I know that he is a valet in disguise, just as we know Magdelon and Cathos are two greenhorns from the provinces trying their best to impress him. Nobody is what he appears to be. It is the beginning of Molière's long preoccupation with the mask.

What Molière is satirising here is not the real thing, but the would-be's. In this sense they are universal types. In any society there tends to be an

[1] Some critics have seen in this name an allusion to Madame de Rambouillet, whose name was Catherine de Vivonne, just as Magdelon has been identified with Madeleine de Scudéry. It seems highly unlikely, however, that Molière, at the very beginning of his career in Paris, would have gone out of his way to antagonise two most influential people.

'in-group', familiarity with which seems more important to some people than genuine talent. To Magdelon, you will remember, knowing all the latest literary gossip seemed much more desirable than real wit. She and her cousin are confusing the external trappings with the real thing. They want to have all the right catch-phrases, but the substance escapes them. They aspire to be highbrows, but without having the essential qualities of mind. You might find their equivalent today at any literary party, or first night, or fashionable opening of an art exhibition. The girls' main interest is to be known, to be seen, to be *there*.

At the same time, they are lamentably unfamiliar with the literary scene. Their ignorance, not to say their innocence, is total. Magdelon confides to Mascarille, 'Unfortunately we are not known yet, but we are getting on, and we have a special friend who has promised to bring all the gentlemen of the *Recueil des Pièces Choisies* to visit us.' This of course refers (Magdelon has muddled the titles) to the two best known precious anthologies of the day with works by all the most popular writers alive and dead, but Magdelon really envisages them all coming to visit her in her *salon*. Her conversation is the oddest mixture of high-flown phrases and crashing ineptitudes. We are continually being reminded that these two girls are in fact 'deux pecques provinciales' who are acting a part, though as the play progresses we can see them becoming more and more carried away by their own performance and convincing themselves that they are real *précieuses*. Mascarille, needless to say, leads them on.

Ridiculous as they are, we are perhaps a little sorry for them when their downfall comes, after their great flights of imagination. They are so naïve, and they are not in any sense corrupt, as Tartuffe is corrupt. Their only crime is to be young and romantic, vain and credulous, and their eventual humiliation seems unnecessarily harsh. This is, however, more a twentieth- than a seventeenth-century point of view. Molière's audience certainly would not have sentimentalised over them. They liked and expected a certain amount of brutality in a play of this kind, which had its roots in farce.

The fact that the girls are far from being what they so ardently desire and pretend to be presents us with a situation full of comic possibilities. With the entry of the next pair of characters, our two knaves, we see the development of these possibilities.

Mascarille comes first. It is probably fair to say that in spite of the title of the play, Mascarille is really the central character. The part was played by Molière himself. He had twice before used the name Mascarille (a traditional one from the *commedia dell'arte*, meaning Little Mask) for a valet, in *l'Étourdi* and *Le Dépit amoureux*, but though the name is the same, the character is different. It was not until *Les Précieuses ridicules* that he developed the part into one which was to become immensely popular with Paris audiences, the caricature of the foppish *marquis*.

Imagine his entry, and the impact it must have made on that first-night audience. Carried in a sedan-chair, he bursts upon the stage making the maximum amount of pother and to-do about how his delicate self has been bumped on the journey. Now he steps out of the chair, and we see him in the full glory of his magnificently absurd costume. Mlle Desjardins has left us a description of it—the towering wig which swept the floor when he bowed, and the tiny hat carried in his hand; a collar so large that it was more like a cape, and lace frills below the knee volumi-nous enough for children to play hide-and-seek in. Ribbons cascaded from his pocket and bows covered his shoes, whose heels were so high that they seemed scarcely to bear the weight of all his finery and powder.

The character was an instant success, as we know from much con-temporary evidence, and probably outweighed the two *précieuses* in popularity. 'J'ose même avancer . . . que les précieuses qui sont dans sa pièce appelées de ce nom, n'en sont pas toute la beauté et que le caractère du marquis de Mascarille, qui est de son invention . . . est une des choses la plus ingénieuse qui ait jamais paru au théâtre et la plus spirituelle de sa pièce.'[2]

The success was no doubt due in large measure to Molière's acting. It was a personal triumph. Under Scaramouche he had perfected the art of gesture and of inspired imitation, so that the comic force of the character probably derived as much from this study of mime as from the verbal wit which he wrote into the part. We must not lose sight of the fact that at this stage of his career Molière was still much more an actor than an author. We tend to think of him now as the great dramatist and prober of human foibles and frailties, but this was all still to come. To Molière's contemporaries, he was an actor. La Grange, who knew him so well says:

[2] François Donneau, preface to *La Cocue imaginaire*, 1660.

Il n'était pas seulement inimitable dans la manière dont il soutenait tous les caractères de ses comédies; mais il leur donnait encore un agrément tout particulier par la justesse qui accompagnait le jeu des acteurs. Un coup d'œil, un pas, un geste, tout y était observé avec une exactitude qui avait été inconnue jusque-là sur les théâtres de Paris.[3]

The character of the ridiculous *marquis* became identified with Molière, and appears in a number of his later plays. In *L'Impromptu de Versailles* (1663), Molière's wife expresses surprise that he is still using the *marquis* as a figure of comedy, to which he replies:

'Que diable voulez-vous que l'on prenne pour un caractère agréable de théâtre? Le marquis aujourd'hui est le plaisant de la comédie; et comme dans toutes les comédies anciennes on voit toujours un valet bouffon qui fait rire les auditeurs, de même dans toutes nos pièces de maintenant il faut toujours un marquis ridicule qui divertisse la compagnie.' (Scene I)

In the same episode, we learn that Molière played the part in a high, light voice.

From the old traditional valet-figure of farce, either rascal or poltroon, Molière has developed Mascarille into a marvellous caricature of the fop and the snob with literary pretensions. Bad poem and fatuous comment alike are gleefully exposed. (The bad poet was to become one of Molière's favourite butts.) It was a contemporary type easily recognisable, but Molière has written in an escape clause. No one can accuse him of making fun of the aristocracy (though *marquis* seem to have been considered legitimate victims), because after all Mascarille is only a dressed-up valet. So the character, from the theatrical point of view, is endowed with the best of both worlds—the knavery of the valet, which is what the audience expected of someone with this name, and the element of social satire, which gave it its new dimension.

With the entry of Jodelet, the tone of the play alters perceptibly. While Mascarille holds the centre of the stage, he is the complete fop and dabbler in literature. As soon as Jodelet comes along, the mood changes and they become two old soldiers bragging about their campaigns (real campaigns, incidentally, which had taken place within the last

[3] Preface to the edition of 1682.

twenty years). There is nothing specifically precious about Jodelet. He is simply being himself, the famous old farce actor who was almost an institution in the French theatre. His real name was Julien Bedeau, and he was a brother of the actor l'Espy who played Gorgibus, but Jodelet was the name by which he was known to generations of Parisians. He had only recently joined Molière's company when he played in *Les Précieuses ridicules*, and he was not destined to be long with it. He died in the following spring, when he was a year or two short of sixty.

His name alone must have been a big draw. A number of farces had been written for him, with titles like *Jodelet ou le Maître Valet* (Scarron) *Jodelet astrologue* (d'Ouville), *Jodelet prince* (Thomas Corneille), and *La Feinte Mort de Jodelet* (Brécourt). It was the familiar Jodelet whom the public wanted to see, with his well-known nasal voice, his 'triste figure', and his 'visage de dogue' heavily whitened in the tradition of farce, so this is how we have to imagine him at that first performance. We may also fairly assume that in the early performances the dialogue in Jodelet's scenes would have varied a little. No doubt he brought with him some of his stock-in-trade of jokes and his own brand of broad humour. Some of the rather crude *double entendres* that survive seem to indicate this, and no doubt Molière allowed for some ad-libbing by Jodelet, who was well known for his ability in this direction.

iii Jargon

Much of the comic effect of *Les Précieuses ridicules* springs from the ridiculous language. The joke was a good one in Molière's own day. The absurd jargon was seized upon with joy by his first audiences, and is still probably the thing which most people think about first in connection with the play. Someone who may know very little else about Molière's *Précieuses* will have heard of the jargon and perhaps be able to quote a phrase or two of it, and this has done much to obscure the fact that basically the satire is directed against the absurdity of pretending to be what one is not, while the much-discussed language is really an incidental, though highly successful, embellishment.

Molière was far from being the first to make fun of affectations in women's speech. In an amusing dialogue entitled *La Ruelle mal assortie*, collected and published by Charles Sorel in 1644, a high-born literary lady gives her handsome but inarticulate Gascon lover a lesson in how to address her in polished phrases:

> Suis-je pas cet adorateur de vos graces, qui ne respire que votre nom, et qui étant en action perpétuelle de désirer ce que je vois et d'admirer tout ce que j'ois, suis ravi de tant de merveilles que je ne sais lequel être, ou d'être tout yeux pour vous regarder, ou pour vous ouïr tout oreilles.

To which the Gascon mumbles in reply 'Bous me l'abez ôté de la vouche!'

Already in 1640 François de Grenailles[4] had remarked with disapproval on the new terms current among women. Interest in language and especially in neologisms was high throughout the seventeenth century. In the years before Molière's comedy Vaugelas[5] (in 1647 and 1657), Sorel[6] (in 1644, 1654 and 1658) and Furetière[7] (1658) had commented on some of these. In 1659 René Bary had published his *Rhétorique française* which contains a long list of new expressions. As the word *précieuse* came

[4] *L'honnête Fille*, p. 26.
[5] *Remarques sur la langue française* (2 edns.).
[6] *Les Loix de la Galanterie* (2 edns.) and *Discours sur l'Académie française*.
[7] *Nouvelle allégorique ou Histoire des Derniers Troubles arrivés au Royaume d'Eloquence.*

into general use, the invention of fashionable or striking phrases tended
to be attributed to them, though in fact there is a remarkable dearth of
evidence to support the idea that the *précieuses* had invented a completely
new jargon, or that there was ever a *préciosité ridicule* of the kind Molière
offers for our entertainment. There seems to be no very clear distinction
between fashionable or society expressions and specifically precious
ones. In general one has the impression that one writer repeats another
about the *précieuses*, saying what the public expected to hear. Be that as
it may, it is apparent that Molière, far from launching a surprise attack,
is simply following the trend of popular opinion about that half-
mythical creature, the *précieuse*.

He does, however, provide a wealth of example of allegedly precious
language, and the question which arises is, how far is it authentic?
The answer emerges when we take the jargon to pieces to see how it is
constructed.

To begin with, we may notice that while Mascarille and the girls
both speak a comic and unlikely language, it is not the same kind.
Mascarille is in fact speaking the language of the novelists and letter-
writing manuals of forty years before; or, to be more exact, the opening
and closing speeches of his big scene (*ix*) are in this style. This is just
sufficient to set the tone; in the rest of the scene, where Mascarille is
leading the girls on with promises of introductions to the literary world,
or making fun of Molière's rivals at the Hôtel de Bourgogne, his language is the speech, barely exaggerated, of a fashionable gentleman of his
day. His opening remarks, however, calculated to set the audience
laughing, are in the style of the novelists Nervèze or des Escuteaux:
'Que craignez-vous?' asks Cathos, and Mascarille replies

> Quelque vol de mon cœur, quelque assassinat de ma franchise. Je vois
> ici deux yeux qui ont la mine d'être de fort mauvais garçons, de faire
> insulte aux libertés et de traiter une âme de Turc à More. Comment,
> diable! d'abord qu'on les approche, ils se mettent sur leur garde
> meurtrière?...

With its absurd weight of metaphor and conceits, Mascarille's speech
could have come straight from one of the novels of the early years of the
century, or from *Le Courtisan Parfait* where compliments of this order
are offered as models: 'Les escopettes de votre beauté brûlent assez le

pourpoint de mon âme, sans que le canon de votre rigueur brise les os de mes prétentions.'[8] Molière has made the style doubly ridiculous by inserting into the middle of Mascarille's grandiloquence two phrases with a popular flavour, 'mauvais garçons' and 'traiter de Turc à More'. As crowning absurdity, he makes Mascarille actually use this kind of language as normal conversation, whereas of course it was a purely literary style.

The scene ends with a return to metaphorical language, when Mascarille, in the middle of a discussion about fashionable clothes, suddenly begins to cry

Ahi! ahi! ahi! doucement. . . . Quoi! toutes deux contre mon cœur en même temps! m'attaquer à droite et à gauche! Ah! c'est contre le droit des gens: la partie n'est pas égale, et je m'en vais crier au meurtre.

What Molière is parodying here is not the conversation of the *salons*, but the literary extravagances of a bygone era. In the same way, his absurd 'impromptu' is a parody of a song in *La Fleur des Chansons nouvelles* of 1614 which contains the lines

> *O voleur! ô voleur! ô voleur!*
> *Rends-moi mon cœur que tu m'as pris.*

In this he was on perfectly safe ground, since it was already the fashion to ridicule the tropes and ornaments of the early years of the century. Gaultier-Garguille, from the rival Hôtel de Bourgogne company, used to make fun of them:

> *Si le vilebrequin de vos yeux*
> *N'eût estocadé, furieux,*
> *Le vieux paletot de mon âme,*
> *Le serrurier de ma douleur*
> *Ne vous ouvrirait pas, Madame,*
> *La fauconnerie de mon cœur, . . .*

and Furetière, in his *Nouvelle allégorique* published the year before

---

[8] *Le Courtisan parfait, enrichi de plusieurs belles et rares lettres de compliments et d'un bouquet de marguerites et fleurs d'élite, choisies dans leur jardin. Finalement multiplié de plusieurs belles et exquises sentences, propos, rodomontades espagnoles et autres.* Amsterdam, 1640, p. 167.

Molière's play, makes Nervèze and des Escuteaux colonels in the battalion of the metaphors in the army of discredited literary devices. Molière, far from breaking new ground, is simply reflecting in his comedy the trend of changing taste.

In the case of Magdelon and Cathos, the picture is different. They do indeed use the expressions of ladies of fashion of their own day, and had Molière wanted ready-made lists of these for inspiration in compiling his jargon, he would not have had far to seek, since, as we have seen, there were at least six works published in the years just before his comedy which cited many of the new expressions. In the second edition of Sorel's *Loix de la Galanterie* (1658), for example, we read that in fashionable speech it was not done to say 'Il a de l'esprit'; if, however, one wished to use the phrase, it was necessary to add 'infiniment', or even something like 'Il a de l'esprit infiniment, et de l'esprit du beau monde et du monde civilisé.' Molière has seized upon this affectation:

—Il a de l'esprit comme un démon
—Et du galant, et du bien tourné.   (Scene xi)

The word *tourné*, incidentally, used in this sense, is another neologism remarked upon by Sorel, and it occurs more than once in the play.

The grotesque effect in the speech of Magdelon and Cathos is produced by density. Their conversation is thick with fashionable phrases like 'du dernier beau', 'le moyen de' (for *comment*) or 'donner dans'; they use the modish plural in expressions like 'Il y a toutes les apparences du monde', and they constantly resort to the exaggerated adverbs 'furieusement', 'effroyablement' and 'terriblement'. (The same procedure is used again in the anonymous *Dialogue de la Mode et de la Nature*, published in 1662, where Fashion speaks a jargon made almost incomprehensible by the cramming together of fashionable locutions.) It is 'society' language in general which Molière is lampooning here. These expressions were not confined to the *précieuses*: indeed Molière uses them again later for other characters, putting them into the mouths of a 'marquise façonnière' (in *L'Impromptu*) and of Harpagon ironically addressing his son.

The fashions of 1659, both sartorial and verbal, were good material for a topical entertainment, and when they could be combined in one phrase, so much the better. Magdelon's 'C'est Perdrigeon tout pur' is an echo of Scarron, who in the same year made a *précieuse* reply, when asked how she had spent the day, 'Oh, ma chère, Bastonneau tout pur.'[9] Perdrigeon and Bastonneau both kept fashionable shops. The remark has the air of a joke which was going the rounds of Paris in that year.

Molière took comic material where he found it. Some of his 'precious' expressions come, directly or indirectly, from Latin authors. Brunot[10] has pointed out that 'le conseiller des grâces' is an echo of Martial, and 'les inclémences de la saison pluvieuse' of Justin. In Molière's own century, Jean Louis Guez de Balzac[11] was a fruitful source of fashionable phraseology. The use of the adjective as a noun ('le vrai de la chose', 'le doux de la flatterie') much favoured by Magdelon and Cathos, is a stylistic device of Balzac ('... de l'attention et de la seconde vue qui polissent le rude et démêlent le confus.' *Aristippe*). This predilection for the substantivised adjective does indeed seem to have been a characteristic of the *précieuses*; at least it features in moderation in the conversations reported by the abbé de Pure, and no doubt it reflects the taste of the *ruelles* for abstraction and delicate distinctions. Molière's two heroines exaggerate it to the absurd: 'C'est là savoir le fin des choses, le grand fin, le fin du fin' (Magdelon, Scene ix).

Besides simple exaggeration, Molière has other jargon-producing tricks. One is to take two fashionable locutions and jumble them together into a nonsense like 'donner de notre sérieux dans le doux de votre flatterie.' Another is to take a neologism not in itself ridiculous: 'Que son intelligence est épaisse' and make it sound so by adding to it: 'et qu'il fait sombre dans son âme.' (Cathos, Scene v.)

Figures of speech abound, and they are made more absurd by being crowded together in close succession: in the first few lines of Scene ix you will find metaphors drawn from hunting, the law, card games and fencing. Again, a figurative expression is made grotesque by using it as a synonym for the common word. Thus, while it is absurd to say, like Magdelon, 'Voiturez-nous ici les commodités de la conversation', one can readily imagine a *précieuse* saying laughingly 'Les fauteuils sont les

9 Letter to Marigny, 8 May 1659.
10 *Histoire de la langue française*, Vol. III, p. 252 (1966 edn.)
11 *Cf.* 'M. de Gomberville se plaint qu'on ait quitté le bon style pour prendre un style de cour. Il dit que Balzac est auteur du style des Précieuses, que sans Molière on allait parler de la sorte.' *Recueil de choses diverses composé vers* 1675, Bib. Nat. Ms. Nouv. acq. fr. 4333, f° 30–31r.

commodités de la conversation' (*commodités* was the normal seventeenth-century word for household equipment). The *salons* had a taste for epigrammatic remarks of this kind; they helped to produce the *Maximes* of La Rochefoucauld, whose wit was polished in the *salon* of Mme de Sablé. Molière, however, is concerned only with making his audience laugh, and this substitution of a figure of speech for the common word is an effective method.

While such procedures are easy to identify, and are as amusing today as when they were written, we should remember that there is also much in this jargon which would have been funny to Molière's audience, but has not the same impact for us, because many expressions which were new at the time have now passed into the language. The word *pousser*, for example, used figuratively, was an innovation. Bouhours, in his *Entretiens d'Ariste et d'Eugène* (1671) remarks on it: 'Pousser est nouveau dans une certaine signification. Pousser les gens à bout . . . pousser une matière . . . cela est trop poussé.' Thus when Cathos says 'Voilà qui est poussé dans le dernier galant', she crams three neologisms into one short sentence. Bouhours also cites *gâter* and *soutenir* as new and forceful figures of speech. Magdelon uses both: 'Vous en êtes l'enfant gâté' and 'Soutenons notre réputation'. Many are derived from Balzac, and Molière has made good use of them. Among these are *sécheresse* (Cathos: 'Quelle sécheresse de conversation') *incongru* (Cathos: 'des gens . . . incongrus en galanterie') and *antipode* (Magdelon: 'l'antipode de la raison.') Though we still catch the note of affectation which Molière has given them, we miss the comic effect of their novelty.

Perhaps the best example of comedy based on the exaggerated use of a neologism, which is rather lost to us today, is in the play Molière makes with the word *air*. The figurative use of the word, as in *avoir l'air de* was new in the seventeenth century. There are comments on it by a number of writers, including Bouhours, and de Pure claims that it is a 'terme de Précieuse'. Expressions such as 'le bel air' or 'l'air galant' were very fashionable, and Molière makes good use of them for comic effect in this and later plays. (In *L'Impromptu*, he instructs La Grange, as a *marquis*, how to make his entry: 'Souvenez-vous bien, vous, de venir . . . là, avec cet air qu'on nomme le bel air, peignant votre perruque et grondant une petite chanson entre vos dents.')

We see then that he is punning when he makes La Grange say in the first scene of *Les Précieuses* 'L'air précieux n'a pas seulement infecté Paris, il s'est aussi répandu dans les provinces, et nos donzelles en ont humé leur bonne part.' The joke is carried a little further in Scene iv when Magdelon says 'Vous devriez un peu vous faire apprendre le bel air des choses', and Gorgibus replies 'Je n'ai que faire ni d'air ni de chanson.' Cathos goes on to complain that La Grange and Du Croisy 'n'ont point cet air qui donne d'abord bonne opinion des gens' and later Magdelon will assure Mascarille that the exaggerated frills on his legs 'ont tout à fait bon air'. The pun on the two meanings of *air* is revived when Mascarille, after claiming that 'tout ce que je fais a l'air cavalier' offers to sing his impromptu for them: 'Je veux vous dire l'air que j'ai fait dessus ... écoutez, si vous trouverez l'air à votre goût.' One imagines the inflection of Mascarille's voice, inviting laughter. Cathos and Magdelon are ecstatic: 'Ah! que voilà un air qui est passionné!' ... 'Je suis enthousiasmée de l'air et des paroles.' Without the knowledge that *air* in the sense of appearance or manner was a new and fashionable term, we would miss the point of Molière's sustained joke.

This famous jargon, then, far from being authentic, is a hotch-potch of comic procedures; principally it is a mixture of baroque literary elegances parodied as conversation, of neologisms and currently fashionable phrases in absurd juxtaposition, and of mutilated epigrams. At the same time Molière contrives to give it a spurious air of authenticity by the inclusion of half-truths and by the distortion of genuine usage. The fact that Somaize pillaged many of these expressions from Molière and included them in his *Dictionnaire des Précieuses* has tended to confirm their appearance of authenticity for posterity, and they are to be found seriously quoted as examples of precious language.

By contrast, the conversation of de Pure's *précieuses* is nothing like this. They speak normal French, made piquant by the inclusion of a few picturesque or humorous new expressions. A visitor to the *ruelles* frequented by de Pure would not have come away with the impression that he had been listening to jargon. De Pure's *précieuses* are interested principally in ideas and in discussion, and language is simply a vehicle for this. Molière's two ninnies, however, have only one idea, which is to succeed in society, and much of the humour springs from the disparity between their high-flown language and their shallow opinions and fatuous remarks.

We can see the technician of comedy at work behind this absurd language. Molière delighted in jargon, and he was an inspired inventor of it, whether it were the mock-Turkish and other nonsense which so impressed M. Jourdain, or the absurd medical jargon of *Le Malade imaginaire*. There is no reason to suppose that we were ever intended to give any more credence to the nonsense spoken by these would-be *précieuses* than to the mumbo-jumbo of the doctors.

iv Mask and Means

We have seen how Molière draws comedy from the jargon which forms a memorable part of the play, but is not the real basis of the comic situation. Fundamentally *Les Précieuses ridicules*, like some of Molière's later plays, is a study in falsity. The four principal characters are all attempting to pass themselves off as something which they are not. Mascarille and Jodelet deceive the girls into believing that they are fine gentlemen, while Magdelon and Cathos attempt to deceive them into believing that they are cultivated young ladies ripe for entry into precious society. Perhaps the element of self-deception enters here too, since the girls are completely carried away by their game of make-believe, and it is difficult to decide where conscious deception ends and self-deception begins.

The high comedy of Scene ix is based on the practised fraud of that name-dropping rascal Mascarille, and on the effort which his victims expend, in vain, trying to make an impression on him. René Bray believes that 'est précieuse une femme d'esprit qui cherche à être femme d'esprit. La préciosité implique . . . toujours l'effort.'[12] The best *précieux* and *précieuses* concealed any effort which went into their productions or their conversation. They valued lightness, sparkle and grace, and anything which smacked of effort was anathema to them. Magdelon and Cathos, however, were poor copies of the real thing, and effort is all too apparent in their conversation.

Molière, as the evidence of the visiting Dutch *savant* Huyghens[13] testifies, at first played the part of Mascarille wearing a mask, in the Italian manner. This, a concession to tradition, was later discarded, and he simply darkened his eyebrows and moustache to give the character that air of stylised absurdity which farce demanded. Mascarille's real mask is a verbal one. He belongs less to the *commedia dell' arte* than to Molière's gallery of characters whose mask is in their speech and actions.

In 1659 Molière was on the threshold of his career as a dramatist, and in *Les Précieuses ridicules* we see the beginning of his long preoccupation with pretence and false appearance. The masks people wear, for one reason or

[12] *La Préciosité et les précieux de Thibaut de Champagne à Jean Giraudoux*, p. 139.

[13] *Journal de voyage de Christian Huyghens*, entry for 20 January 1661.

another, are his abiding interest, and he is adept at showing us the person behind them. It has been suggested that this reflects the situation in the court-dominated society of Molière's day where all were compelled by etiquette 'to assume the mask, to act a part, to keep up their social rôle . . . what is politeness but a cloak, a mask thrown over self-interest?'[14]

While Mascarille struts and postures as the aristocrat-cum-salon poet, Magdelon and her cousin don the mask of culture. Their deception is rather less successful. The mask constantly slips, revealing the ingenuous girls up from the country who really believe that 'all these gentlemen of the *Recueil des Pièces Choisies*' will come to visit them. In imitating the externals of culture without any conception of its essence, they are ridiculous. Molière develops the comedy of this idea in other plays. M. Jourdain believes that he will become a gentleman by acquiring a smattering of the social accomplishments, and Orgon, as H. Gaston Hall has pointed out, might be called a 'dévot ridicule' because he imitates the externals of piety without understanding its inner meaning.[15] Over the years, Molière will build up a study of this kind of character.

A play in which the principal people wear the mask of an assumed personality must inevitably depend for its *dénouement* upon their un-masking, and so it is in *Les Précieuses ridicules*. In later comedies dramatic exposure takes place in a less visual manner, but farce asserts itself here, and the tearing away of the false personalities is simple and physical—the valets are literally stripped of their finery on the stage, no doubt to the huge delight of that first audience.

'Le premier, l'immense mérite de Molière est d'avoir trouvé et fixé la matière de la comédie, savoir: la vie,' wrote Gustave Rudler[16] nearly fifty years ago. Attitudes of mind, self-deceptions, fantasies, kinds of behaviour which are common to us all, these are the stuff of his comedy. Yet often these same things do not appear ridiculous to us until we see them in his characters. Molière was once asked why this should be so:

[14] W. G. Moore, *Molière, A New Criticism*, p. 39.

[15] *Tartuffe*, in this series, p. 24.

[16] From a script published after Professor Rudler's death by Dr. W. G. Moore at the end of his tribute to him in *French Studies*, January 1958, Vol. XII, p. 3.

Nous lui demandâmes pourquoi le même ridicule, qui nous échappe
souvent dans l'original, nous frappe à coup sûr dans la copie. Il nous
répondit que c'est parce que nous le voyons alors avec les yeux de
l'imitateur qui sont meilleurs que les nôtres; car, ajouta-t-il, le talent
n'est pas donné à tout le monde.[17]

His comedy springs not simply from the actions of the characters, as
in farce and earlier comedy, but from the revelation of the inner pre-
occupations which motivate those actions. This is more highly developed
in the later plays than in *Les Précieuses ridicules*; nevertheless it is apparent
here too. Somaize and Gilbert also wrote comedies about the *précieuses*,
and no one reads them now. Why is it that their heroines are paste-
board figures, while Magdelon and Cathos are genuinely comic characters? Is it not because in Molière's play we are constantly aware of the
immense, the impossible gap between the heroines' ambition and their
performance? The comedy of the situation is heightened by the fact that
the gap is not at all apparent to them. They are convinced that they are
making an excellent impression. This gulf between fact and fantasy,
between the dream and its realisation, is something which Molière will
exploit as a source of comedy in a number of his later plays. Arnolphe is
the next in the succession of characters whose dreams come into sharp
conflict with reality.

Nothing which will produce comedy is disdained in this play. Puns
abound—Gorgibus, as we might expect, is fond of them, and Jodelet has
the most absurd one: 'Je me trouve un peu incommodé de la veine
poétique, pour la quantité de saignées que j'y ai fait faire ces jours
passés.' The trick of rendering a syllable or phrase ridiculous by repetition
('Oh! oh! Voilà qui est extraordinaire: oh! oh!' etc.) will reappear in
many of the later plays, and here, of course, the comic effect depends
upon the voice. Actor that he was, Molière knew the value of visual
comedy too. Mascarille's appearance, as we have seen, made a lasting
impression on Parisian audiences. Exaggeration and distortion, of ideas
as well as of speech, add to the comedy. The famous delicacy of the
précieuses in matters of taste and sensibility becomes immediately laughter-
provoking when it is translated into the terms of Cathos' appalled
exclamation: 'Comment est-ce qu'on peut souffrir la pensée de coucher

[17] Abbé de Châteauneuf, *Dialogue sur la musique*, 1725; but the
conversation took place 'peu de jours avant qu' il donnât son Tartuffe'.

contre un homme vraiment nu!' There is a kind of humour which elicits a smile and another which produces a guffaw. Both have their part in *Les Précieuses ridicules*.

Much of the comedy is produced by a series of confrontations. It begins as we saw with a clash between the generations in which the protagonists represent not good sense on the one hand and folly on the other, but rather opposite extremes of absurdity. Gorgibus is as ridiculous as the girls. With Mascarille's arrival the pattern changes to the time-honoured confrontation of knave and fool, the funnier because the whole episode is enacted in an atmosphere of exaggerated politeness. In this (Scene ix), one of the most successful comic scenes Molière ever wrote, we have the added joy of witnessing a double deception. The girls, striving to pass themselves off as literary ladies, are themselves dupes of the false *marquis*.

Before the spectacle of the two sillies being gulled by the wily Mascarille has had time to pall a new element is introduced, and the swash-buckling 'vicomte de Jodelet' arrives as a foil for the foppish *marquis*. The ultra-delicacy of Scene ix is replaced by its opposite in Scene xi, where innuendo and gesture provide comedy of a different order.

Finally, in the last scenes, comes the inevitable clash between fantasy and stern reality, when the house of cards comes tumbling down, *marquis* and *vicomte* are again servants beaten by their masters, and the erstwhile *précieuses*, far from entertaining a *salon* full of notable people, are upbraided and ignominiously sent upstairs to hide their faces.

In a more complicated comedy, with more agreeable characters, there would still be loose ends to be tied up, lovers to be united and so on, but in *Les Précieuses ridicules*, as in the older farces, no character is particularly sympathetic, and the action can conclude with the unmasking of the valets, the discomfiture of the *précieuses*, and, for good measure, a few hearty thwacks to the innocent musicians. It is indicative of the change in taste that this last scene with Gorgibus and the musicians is often suppressed in modern productions, so that the play ends with Mascarille's rueful but waggish comment.

Let it not be suggested that these clashes and confrontations, or any of the other technicalities of the comedy, were the result of planning. It is infinitely more probable that they sprang from the instinctive feeling for what would succeed on the stage, which came from Molière's years of training on the boards. As an actor, he had to face the immediate personal reaction of audiences, and uninhibited audiences at that. He knew, from the most direct kind of experience, what would keep them amused.

If by holding up a distorting mirror to the life of the *salons* he can make people laugh, that is enough. (He will repeat the successful joke in later comedies.) As social comment the play has bite without profundity. The fashionable world and the would-be literary set are ridiculed, but as Molière himself says of his comedy 'elle se tient partout dans les bornes de la satire honnête et permise' (Preface). Exaggeration and distortion are legitimate means of producing comedy. Grimarest, looking back many years later on the first production of *Les Précieuses ridicules*, commented that 'Molière connaissait déjà le point de vue du théâtre, qui demande de gros traits pour affecter le public, et ce principe lui a toujours réussi dans tous les caractères qu'il a voulu peindre.'[18]

[18] *Vie de Molière*, edited by Mongrédien, 1955, p. 48.

v Comic Vision

It is tempting, in the case of *Les Précieuses ridicules*, to dwell on the social background of the play, if only for the reason that here Molière is portraying, or rather parodying, a unique and interesting aspect of life in the seventeenth century. But the play has an importance and an interest which go far beyond this. Any study of the nature of Molière's comedy must come back, as its starting-point, to his *Précieuses*. If we go beyond the immediate comic effect to the underlying principle of comedy, we shall see how Magdelon and Cathos join hands with the later, greater, and more minutely presented characters.

In this short comedy we find, as it were in miniature, not only much of Molière's dramatic art but, more important, the first indication of a theme of comedy which he will explore in depth, and from all angles, in the course of the next fourteen years. Reduced to its simplest terms, it is the conflict between theory and life itself. The blind theorist, the man with a fixed idea, the man possessed by some form of mono-mania is, for Molière, *par excellence* a subject of comedy. From year to year and from play to play he will explore the effect of this kind of ruling passion on the man himself and on his relations with other people.[19] On one level, it provides pure comedy in individual scenes. Orgon, presented with an account of his wife's troubles, hears and thinks of nothing but what is preoccupying him: 'Et Tartuffe?' Against all evidence and reason, he will continue to exclaim: 'Le pauvre homme!' On a deeper level, Molière explores the dehumanising effect on the man himself of his dominating idea. He specialises in the study of people in whom something is, to a greater or lesser degree, somehow askew. Most of them are men, but there are exceptions: the *précieuses* are the first of these, the comtesse d'Escarbagnas, with the *femmes savantes*, the last.

Magdelon and Cathos have been called 'pédantes de l'amour'.[20] Theorists of love, they recoil from the reality, not only, it would seem, because a conventional arranged marriage such as Gorgibus has planned for them is 'du dernier bourgeois', but also, and more important,

[19] *Cf.* Valdemar Vedel: 'Son comique, sa satire, sont issus d'un instinct des plus profonds et des plus sensibles de ce qui nuit aux relations humaines.' *Deux classiques français*, 1935, p. 504.

[20] Marcel Gutwirth, *Molière ou l'invention comique*, 1966, p. 82.

because their whole conception of what marriage is about is based on theory, and patently absurd theory at that. The conventions of the romantic novel have as little relation to reality as the poetic convention beloved by the baroque poets that the fair Sylvie, Iris and the rest were all ice and snow. Magdelon and Cathos are confusing the real with the empty form, and rejecting the substance for the shadow. Molière makes splendid comedy from Magdelon's long statement of how a relationship between a man and a woman should develop. 'Il faut,' she begins, speaking of the ideal lover, 'que sa recherche soit dans les formes.' It is Molière's first round in the series of attacks he will make on those who adhere strictly to rules and forms, leading up to the ultimate absurdity of: 'Il vaut mieux mourir selon les règles, que de réchapper contre les règles.'[21]

Formal doctrine of all kinds, medical, literary, legal, all come under attack at various times. In particular, those who seek to live by formula seem to be of special interest to Molière, and the more so when their formula sets them above or apart from ordinary human beings. In this, two different kinds of comedy meet, and the *Précieuses* join the *Misanthrope*. Neither can accept the world as it is. For his *Précieuses*, the commonplaces of daily life must be veiled in verbiage, and the realities of marriage indefinitely postponed. Life itself will slip away from them while they are theorising about the ideal courtship. The sources of their 'apartness' from the rest of humanity, however, are different. In the case of Magdelon and Cathos, naïve and uncomplicated characters, it is dictated by misplaced ambition and the misapplication of the formula of the novel to real life; in Alceste, the source is something deeper in the man himself.

Lionel Gossman makes an interesting division of Molière's comedies into the 'open' type, such as *Les Précieuses ridicules* and *Le Bourgeois gentilhomme*, and the 'closed' type which includes *Le Misanthrope*. The difference lies in the comic hero's relation to the world, since the comic hero 'looks to others to give him his value and his being.' Whereas one group of Molière's characters make no attempt to conceal their admiration for some section of society and their desire to be part of it, those in another group, among whom Alceste, affect to despise the people whose recognition they desire. Gossman remarks that with the

[21] Dr. Bahys in *L'Amour médecin*. Act II, Scene V.

notable exceptions of Don Juan and Jupiter, the majority of Molière's best-known characters are bourgeois, and that there is a distinction between the upper and lower range. In general the first group of characters, those whose vanities and illusions are openly avowed, like the *précieuses*, come from the lower bourgeoisie and provinces, while the second group, who make a point of scorning the ways of the world, come from the upper bourgeoisie, and their 'vanities and illusions are less easily discerned as comic, for they resemble those we ourselves conceal.[22]

Inevitably, those who seek to live by a formula will come into conflict with real life. Against the formula for living of the *précieuses*, with its emphasis on refinement, ultra-delicacy, and withdrawal from all that they find 'tout à fait choquant', Molière opposes life in the raw, red-blooded, lusty and bawdy, as the two valets typify it. We discern Molière's impatience with all that the attitude of the *précieuses* to life implies. Ramon Fernandez makes this point:

> Or, la préciosité est justement l'art du retard, de l'hésitation devant la hâte amoureuse. C'est même, en fin de compte, l'art de refuser le contact tout en profitant de l'émotion trouble soulevée par le désir. Le langage précieux est une manière d'éviter de toucher les corps, les corps de ces hommes 'vraiment nus' contre lesquels Cathos et Magdelon ne veulent point coucher. Homme et mots 'vraiment nus': voilà ce que la préciosité—celle de Cathos comme celle d'Armande, comme celle, plus subtile et toute provisoire, de Célimène—repousse et recouvre d'un voile que Molière déchire avec une rage allègre. Non par raison et bon sens, comme on l'a dit assez superficiellement, mais pour satisfaire un instinct impérieux et gourmand, une hâte des sens et des muscles qui fait de lui l'ennemi en quelque sorte biologique des superfétations.[23]

Judgment is passed upon them in Scene xi, where Jodelet brings the comedy back to the earthy realities of farce. After the ultra-delicacy which the girls have earlier professed, and their wish for a protracted courtship with its consummation indefinitely postponed ('j'ai mal au cœur de la seule vision que cela me fait'), they are confronted with a travesty of all that they have been extolling. Far from the languishings of

[22] Lionel Gossman, *Men and Masks, a Study of Molière*, 1963, pp. 207–8.
[23] Ramon Fernandez, *Molière*, in *Tableau de la littérature française de Corneille à Chénier*, 1939, p. 87.

an imaginary lover, 'tout rêveur et mélancolique', who is willing to wait indefinitely for 'cet aveu qui fait tant de peine', they are subjected to a brisk campaign by two rascals whose native vulgarity is by this time only too apparent under their fine clothes. 'Il faut qu'un amant, pour être agréable, sache débiter les beaux sentiments, pousser le doux, le tendre et le passionné'—such was Magdelon's formula for her wooing. What a contrast to this theorising is the reality as Molière presents it: two sniggering valets casting bold glances at the girls, and exchanging with each other innuendoes and veiled references to past amatory exploits. It is only at the last minute that Magdelon manages to restrain them from undressing to exhibit 'des marques honorables, qui font voir ce qu'on est.' The irony of the situation is heightened by the fact that the girls, for all their vaunted delicacy, seem totally unaware of what is going on, to the point of greeting a grossly indecent remark by Mascarille with the exclamation: 'Que tout ce qu'il dit est naturel! Il tourne les choses le plus agréablement du monde.' Here, as often in Molière's later comedies, the artificial person is betrayed by the natural person underneath. Tartuffe is betrayed by his sensuality, Magdelon and Cathos by their sheer native stupidity and insensitiveness—by the two qualities, in fact, which are the exact opposite of those they affect to possess in large measure. They have set themselves up as paragons of wit, refinement, delicacy and sensibility, yet they continue, in the face of all evidence, to pour out their praises of the 'marquis'. The sham of their artificially created personalities is exposed in an instant.

The spirit of farce has taken over from the comedy of manners and social satire of the earlier scenes. Les Précieuses ridicules owes its being to the fusion of these two elements. Farce, coarse, earthy, exuberant, vital, is allied to the highly civilised comedy of ideas and finely observed portrayal of human behaviour. It is possible to see Les Précieuses ridicules as a symbol of the meeting of these two extremes, which together form the stuff of Molière's comic genius. What Fernandez calls an instinctive haste, 'un mouvement qui sourd des profondeurs biologiques de l'homme', seems to have been the source of the glee with which Molière exposes his two would-be précieuses to rough reality. In doing so he produces that 'choc exquis' from which comedy springs, that moment of recognition in which, without any moralising, judgment is passed.

Vedel has remarked that Molière uses the actions of farce to symbolise the inner dramatic situation, in the way that ballet provides the visual expression of an interior drama. The same audience which accepted the convention that violent action was banned from the stage in tragedy delighted to see it in comedy and Molière continued, until the end of his life, to make full use of the resources of farce to point his comedy. In *Les Précieuses* we have it in its simplest form. Ridiculous action provides a silent comment on attitudes of mind no less ridiculous. When Mascarille in Scene xii whirls Magdelon into an absurd dance, all the time keeping up his ludicrous monologue ('Ma franchise va danser la courante aussi bien que mes pieds . . .'), we have the perfect comment on the verbal dance he has led her in the earlier scenes, as well as an ironical glance backward at the exaggeratedly high value which the two girls set upon themselves at the beginning of the play. Farcical action at its conclusion—the dance with two valets—provides all the comment we need on the validity of their claims to distinction.

We have seen that those who set themselves apart, in one way or another, from the rest of humanity provide Molière with much of his comic material. In particular, those who, like our *précieuses*, mask mediocrity under an affectation of superiority are his chosen victims. He returns to the attack again, and for the last time, thirteen years later in *Les Femmes savantes*. His learned ladies have this, besides much else, in common with Magdelon and Cathos, that they wish to set aside the natural order of things in favour of 'cette union des cœurs où les corps n'entrent pas', and see themselves as members of a small select group of superior beings: 'Nul n'aura de l'esprit hors nous et nos amis.' It is more than just the new feminine fashion for erudition which Molière is satirising in *Les Femmes savantes*, just as it is more than passing fashions in language which he ridicules in *Les Précieuses*. The source of comedy goes deeper. It is concerned with a whole attitude towards life itself.

III

Molière and the Précieuses

One of the areas of debate in connection with the play is this: how far were Magdelon and Cathos a parody of the real thing? Molière makes it clear from the beginning that his heroines were not real Parisian *précieuses*, and he stresses this in his preface to the published version: '—les plus excellentes choses sont sujettes à être copiées par de mauvais singes . . . aussi les véritables précieuses auraient tort de se piquer lorsqu' on joue les ridicules qui les imitent mal.'

It has been said of course that this was simply a prudent measure to avoid bringing down the wrath of a powerful group on his head. There was, however, nothing resembling an organised group of *précieuses* who felt that the name applied to them, but rather a number of quite separate intelligent, charming, witty women who attracted poets and men of letters to their gatherings.

On the other hand, as we have seen, the word *précieuse* was being bandied about at the time Molière wrote his comedy. He has put into his entertainment some of the ideas which were current about this new creature, notably the idea that she affected a particular jargon. You will remember too that the word was sometimes equated with *prude*, and we have an allusion to this in Cathos' immortal remark. In short he is simply going with the stream of opinion and repeating, though in a much more clever and lively fashion, a joke that was already familiar to the public. This is important to successful light comedy—confirmation of what we have already accepted. We do not really want to be shocked or startled. To these popular notions, Molière has added his own inimitable touch and unerring sense of theatre, and fused them all into a delightful entertainment. For this is how we should look at *Les Précieuses ridicules*, as an entertainment, satirical certainly, but not as a ferocious satire performed with the single purpose of discrediting a movement of which Molière disapproved.

It is true that the title suggests a satire on the *précieuses*, but as Donneau de Visé points out, Molière 'ne se soucie pas que ses pièces aient des noms qui leur conviennent pourvu qu'elles en aient de spécieux et qui puissent exciter de la curiosité.'[1] *Précieuses* was certainly a good word to have in the title of a play in 1659. As far as content goes, however, it might equally well be entitled *Les Pecques jouées*, or even *le Marquis ridicule*, though this is the title of a play by Scarron. While it does undoubtedly satirise some features of preciosity, this is not the whole story.

The satire is on two levels. Basically it ridicules some aspects of human behaviour which are constant. The desire to ape the manners of a higher social class than one's own seems deeply rooted in human nature. Magdelon and Cathos are social climbers of the first order. Their background is provincial bourgeois, not particularly cultivated. The kind of society they are trying to climb into is Parisian, aristocratic and literary. Given this situation, all kinds of affectation and pretension can be pilloried. Mascarille is a marvellous parody of the fashionable and effete snob. From his entry, talking loudly of his next engagement at the Louvre, to his meeting with Jodelet—'Ah, Vicomte! (s'embrassant l'un l'autre)—Ah, Marquis!'—we recognise the type. Magdelon and Cathos are doing their best to shake off their origins. 'Ah! Mon père, ce que vous dites là est du dernier bourgeois', says Magdelon, who would like to believe that she is the natural daughter of some aristocrat. Paris with its 'beau monde' gleams brightly for the girls as 'le centre du bon goût'. They place great value on knowing the latest gossip and the most fashionable shops, second only to the importance of knowing the right people. One part of the joke, then, is at the expense of snobs and social climbers.

The other part is at the expense of the kind of society which the girls are trying to enter, the world of preciosity, and here Molière's gibes are directed especially at shallow intellectual pretensions, second-hand opinions, 'arty' conversation (he returns to the attack on these things in *La Critique de l'Ecole des Femmes*) and modish language. Satirical, certainly, is this picture of the fashionable literary salon set, but satirical in a general way.

It has been claimed, and by eminent critics, that Molière was making a personal attack on Madeleine de Scudéry. The textual justification for this view is that Magdelon says to her father (in Scene iv) 'Mon Dieu! que

[1] Lettre sur les affaires du théâtre, *Diversités galantes*, 1664.

si tout le monde vous ressemblait, un roman serait bientôt fini! La belle chose que ce serait si d'abord Cyrus épousait Mandane, et qu'Aronce de plain-pied fût marié à Clélie', while Cathos observes that anyone who has not heard of the *Carte de Tendre* can hardly be numbered among the Best People. Both girls would like to change their names to ones more suitable to heroines of romance, Polyxène and Aminthe.

But can this be interpreted as an attack on Madeleine de Scudéry? The comedy springs from the absurdity of the girls' confusing real life with Arcadian romance. Molière might as easily have used *Astrée* for the romantic novel, but his comedy is a topical one, and it would be logical to use the novels which everyone was reading and talking about at the time. It is not the works themselves which are held up to ridicule, but rather the girls' literal application of them to their own situation. Molière also mentions Charles de Sercy's *Poésies Choisies de Messieurs Corneille, Benserade, de Scudéry, Boisrobert etc.* and his *Recueil de pièces en prose*. No one has so far suggested that he was launching an attack on all the authors who feature in them.

There seems no reason to suppose that Mlle de Scudéry, leading novelist of the day and presiding genius of the *Samedis*, is to be confused with the silly little girls who have read her romances. We may note in passing that the fashion for drawing fun from the contrast between real life and the implausible situations of novels had already begun long before with Charles Sorel's *Berger Extravagant* (1627), which has a bourgeois hero in trouble through too much reading of *Astrée*. Molière, once again, is not innovating, but incorporating a popular joke.

A more substantial reason for regarding Madeleine de Scudéry as the object of Molière's attack has been advanced by Antoine Adam in his article *La Genèse des Précieuses ridicules*.[2] He suggests that in 1659 certain literary factions were associated with political groups, and sees in this the reason for the acrimony which marked some of their exchanges. He shows that a coterie of former *frondeurs*, associated with Gaston d'Orléans and the Grande Mademoiselle, led by d'Aubignac and consisting of the abbé de Pure, the abbé Cotin,[3] Gilles Boileau, Sauval, Furetière and

[2] *Revue d'histoire de la philosophie et d'histoire générale de la civilisation*, Lille, 1939, pp. 14–46.

[3] Literary alliances were not lasting. Molière's later attack on Cotin as Trissotin is well known. He seems also not to have been a friend of de

D

La Calprenède, was opposed to Mademoiselle de Scudéry and her friends Ménage and Pellisson, *protégés* of Fouquet. Professor Adam believes that on his arrival in Paris Molière aligned himself with d'Aubignac and his group and was inspired by them to write an anti-*précieuse* satire directed primarily against Madeleine de Scudéry. He establishes the link between Molière and this coterie through Mlle Desjardins, a *protégée* of d'Aubignac, and through the fact that Molière jokingly promised on his play-bills another farce to follow *Les Précieuses ridicules*, to be entitled *Ménage hypercritique, le faux savant et le pédant coquet.*

Professor Adam believes that there was a first version of *Les Précieuses* which was a clear attack on Mlle de Scudéry and her friends:

> C'est directement contre Sapho, contre les habitués du *Samedi*, contre les salons amis de Mme du Plessis-Bellière et de Mme du Plessis-Guénégaud, contre Angélique-Clarisse d'Angennes, que Molière a composé *Les Précieuses ridicules*. (p. 44)

He accepts Somaize's statement that the intervention of an unidentified 'alcôviste de qualité' was the cause of a break in performances, and believes that in the interval between the first and second performances Molière altered the play to avoid further trouble, making the heroines into provincial girls and 'fausses précieuses'.

If this theory be correct, it would involve, not merely a few alterations here and there, but a complete re-writing and re-orientation of the comedy, since in the play as we know it the internal necessities both of structure and character demand that the heroines should be naïve and rather stupid provincial girls who might plausibly fall victims to the kind of deception which constitutes the plot. It is impossible to conceive that, unless the play were completely different, one of its heroines could have been identified with Mlle de Scudéry.[4]

We must also accept the fact that, unless fresh evidence comes to light, the whole question of whether or not the play was suspended as a result of some outside intervention must be regarded as not proven.

Pure's, and Lathuillère has shown that 'l'appartenance de l'abbé (de Pure) à la cabale aubignacienne est fort problématique et, tout au moins, éphémère.' *La Préciosité*, 1966, Vol. I, p. 99.

[4] R. Lathuillère (*op. cit.*, pp. 102 *et seq.*) marshals all the arguments against a radically different first version.

The aim of Professor Adam's article is to show that the object of Molière's satire in *Les Précieuses ridicules* was not general but particular. Against this may be placed Molière's own statement of intention, not only in the preface to the *Précieuses*, where his disclaimers could have been dictated by prudence, but also in *L'Impromptu*, where we have his manifesto in the matter:

> Il disait que rien ne lui donnait du déplaisir comme d'être accusé de regarder quelqu'un dans les portraits qu'il fait; que son dessein est de peindre les mœurs sans vouloir toucher aux personnes, et que tous les personnages qu'il représente sont des personnages en l'air, et des fantômes proprement, qu'il habille à sa fantaisie pour réjouir les spectateurs; qu'il serait bien fâché d'y avoir jamais marqué qui que ce soit. (*L'Impromptu de Versailles*, Scene iv)[5]

Whatever Molière's intention may or may not have been in writing *Les Précieuses ridicules*, there is no evidence that Madeleine de Scudéry took his mention of her novels as a personal attack, or that she bore him any rancour; there is, on the other hand, evidence that she praised *Les Fâcheux* and *Tartuffe*.

Molière had no quarrel with women of genuine distinction. His life as an actor would have predisposed him to accept women as equals, for the theatre was the only sphere in which men and women worked together on a footing of equality. In Molière's own troupe the women had an equal voice in matters affecting them all and equal shares in the profits. That he enjoyed the society of genuinely witty women is certain. We have a delightful picture of him and Boileau dining with Ninon de Lenclos and Mme de la Sablière, while Boileau is making up the mock-Latin which features in *le Malade imaginaire*.[6] We know that Molière enjoyed Ninon's lively sense of the ridiculous, and we can imagine the scene of gaiety on that occasion. One critic believes that Molière considered the *galantes* like Ninon to be the real *précieuses*, and the *prudes* to be the false ones.[7]

[5] See also *La Critique de l'Ecole des Femmes*, Scene vi—Uranie: 'Ces sortes de satires tombent directement sur les mœurs et ne frappent les personnes que par réflexion.' etc.

[6] Monchesnay, *Bolaeana*, 1742, p. 34.

[7] E. Magne, *Ninon de Lenclos*, 1927.

Molière's contemporaries had developed a taste for satire, and, according to Donneau de Visé, did not really resent his jokes at their expense:

> Il (Molière) apprit que les gens de qualité voulaient rire à leur dépens, qu'ils voulaient que l'on fît voir leurs défauts en public, qu'ils étaient les plus dociles du monde . . . puisque, loin de se fâcher de ce que l'on eut les Précieuses, où ils étaient et si bien représentés et bien raillés, ils donnèrent eux-mêmes avec beaucoup d'empressement à l'auteur . . . des mémoires de tout ce qui se passait dans le monde et des portraits de leurs propres défauts et de ceux de leurs meilleurs amis.[8]

It became the fashion to invite Molière to dinner and ply him with suggestions as to which contemporary type he should put in his next play. (The King himself suggested the inclusion of the hunting bore in *Les Fâcheux*.) It all sounds very good-humoured. Far from being offended by the *Précieuses*, it seems that the aristocratic intelligentsia took the joke in good part.

Why then has it been claimed that it aroused fierce indignation among the *précieuses*? In essence this is based on the break of a fortnight in performances after the first, which Somaize attributes to the intervention of 'un alcôviste de qualité'. As has already been seen, some scholars believe that during this fortnight the play was altered so that the heroines were made provincial and not Parisian *précieuses*: Professor Adam's theory has been outlined above. The chief factual evidence for an earlier version is Mlle Desjardins' account of the first performance, which differs slightly from the published text. Mlle Desjardins was not, however, present at the first performance. Her account is at second hand, and was intended to entertain a friend, Mme de Morangis. Apart from the fact that Mlle Desjardins believed that the first interview between the suitors and the girls took place on the stage, her account does not differ in any important respect from the play as we know it, though two rather broad jokes which she mentions have been suppressed in the published version.

In the matter of the break in performances, it is noteworthy that another of just over a fortnight occurred the following month, which weakens the case for an enforced suspension, and suggests that there

---

[8] *Nouvelles nouvelles*, 1663.

may have been some more prosaic reason, such as perhaps the illness of an indispensable member of the cast. Jodelet died a few months later, and may well have been in poor health at this time. There are even references to his illness in the text. These are usually interpreted by editors as being a joke about his whitened clown's face, but this does not explain his remark in Scene xii: 'Ne pressez pas si fort la cadence; je ne fais que sortir de maladie.' Molière, as we know, was in the habit of writing his actors' infirmities into the text. La Flèche's limp and his own cough are well-known examples.

If on the other hand we are to accept Somaize's uncorroborated statement that the break was due to an enforced suspension brought about by some powerful 'alcôviste de qualité', we must wonder who he was. The inference is that he intervened because the *précieuses* were incensed; but this supposes that they were an organised group, which we know was not the case. Somaize of course, writing a so-called dictionary of the *précieuses*, constantly bends the facts to fit his purpose, and it would suit him to suggest that the intervention (if intervention there was) was made on behalf of the *précieuses*.

Human nature being what it is, however, it seems probable that there was some less chivalrous reason for it. Who else might have borne a grudge against Molière after that first performance? His rivals at the Hôtel de Bourgogne can hardly have been pleased by his mockery of them, and would probably have been glad to see performances suspended by an *alcôviste de qualité*.

A candidate for this title presents himself in the person of the abbé de Pure. He came, as we saw earlier, of a wealthy and aristocratic family and Somaize, who admired and praised him extravagantly, elsewhere calls him 'un homme de qualité' and notes meaningly that 'il semble qu'il soit né plus pour inventer que pour imiter' (*Grand Dictionnaire*, under *Prospère*). De Pure had connections with the Hôtel de Bourgogne, where his tragedy *Ostorius* had been played in that same year. (Molière's friend Boileau later ridiculed *Ostorius* in his *Dialogue des Héros de Roman* as he had ridiculed de Pure himself in Satires II and IX.) Further, de Pure seems to have shared with Thomas Corneille a low opinion of Molière's company at the Petit-Bourbon.[9] Molière's enemies, as we have seen,

[9] See a letter from Thomas Corneille, in reply to the abbé de Pure, 1 December 1659, in which he is 'fâché . . . que la haute opinion que M. de

accused him of plagiarising de Pure's Italian comedy about the *précieuses*, and since de Pure was still publishing works about them (the last volume of *La Prétieuse* in 1658 and the first part of his unfinished novel *Epigone* in 1659), he and Molière were exploiting the same subject. All in all, there may well have been an element of personal animosity.

This, however, is mere supposition, and rests on the assumption that Somaize is telling the truth when he speaks of the intervention of an *alcôviste de qualité*. Somaize also had connections with the Hôtel de Bourgogne. Its actors probably inspired or commissioned him to compose *Les Véritables Précieuses* (1660) which, besides attacking Molière, praises a number of plays which had recently been performed at the Hôtel de Bourgogne.

All that may be said with certainty is that opposition to Molière's play seems to have come chiefly from rivals in the same field, both authors and actors, while there is remarkably little evidence that any *précieuse* was incensed by it. The final word in the matter was pronounced by Molière himself, who was in a position to know:

> Les Marquis, les Précieuses, les Cocus et les Médecins ont souffert doucement qu'on les ait représentés et ils font semblant de se divertir avec tout le monde des peintures que l'on a faites d'eux, mais les Hypocrites n'ont point entendu raillerie. (Preface to *Tartuffe*, 1669)

The other most often repeated belief, which seems to have arisen towards the end of the century, is that Molière's satire put an end to preciosity. Charles Perrault, writing in 1696, would have us believe that the effect of *Les Précieuses ridicules* was almost magical and that 'toute la nation des précieuses s'éteignit en moins de quinze jours'.[10] Ménage, who was present at the first performance, wrote, many years later:

> La pièce fut jouée avec un applaudissement général, et j'en fus si satisfait en mon particulier que je vis dès lors l'effet qu'elle allait

la Clairière avait du jeu des Messieurs de Bourbon n'ait pas été remplie avantageusement pour lui. Tout le monde dit qu'ils ont joué détestablement sa pièce (*Oreste et Pylade*); et le grand monde qu'ils ont eu à leur farce des *Précieuses*, après l'avoir quittée, fait bien connaître qu'ils ne sont propres qu'à soutenir du semblables bagatelles. . . .' (Bib. Nat. Ms. f. fr. 12763.)

[10] *Les Hommes illustres qui ont paru en France pendant ce Siècle*, Vol. I, p. 80.

produire ... Cela arriva comme je l'avais prédit, et dès cette première représentation l'on revient du galimatias et du style forcé.[11]

The note of self-satisfaction is evident, but it is not borne out by the facts. Things do not happen so tidily, except in the histories of literature. Anthologies of precious writing continued to be compiled, published and republished until the end of the century. The *Recueil La Suze-Pellisson* had sixteen editions between 1663 and 1698, and it was one of many similar collections. The literary *salons* continued to flourish, and feminine fashions and affectations in one form or another continued to provide Molière with material for his later comedies. Twenty years or so after his death, women were still affecting certain new expressions which differed very little in nature from those which had been considered precious in the middle years of the century. Boursault lists some of these in his comedy *Les Mots à la Mode* (1694), and his Babet and Nannette are simply the later counterparts of Magdelon and Cathos, in that their speech is crammed full of new and modish expressions. In short, *Les Précieuses ridicules* made little difference, and when preciosity as the seventeenth century had known it finally came to an end, it was by a gradual process of merging and changing rather than by any *coup de grâce* delivered by Molière.

The idea, which persisted until this century, of Molière as a dedicated reformer bent upon sweeping away abuses, also probably arose towards the end of his own century, when a high moral tone crept into much of its writing, reflecting perhaps the severity of outlook which overtook Louis XIV with advancing years. Typical of the trend is the comment of Bordelon who, while censuring comedy in general, remarks that 'Molière a plus corrigé de défauts à la cour et à la ville que tous les prédicateurs ensemble.'[12] To divert the court and the town, and to keep his company solvent is in fact more likely to have been Molière's real intention than the conscious correction of faults. 'Je voudrais bien savoir si la grande règle de toutes les règles n'est pas de plaire, et si une pièce de théâtre qui a attrapé son but n'a pas suivi un bon chemin'.[13] That *Les Précieuses ridicules* followed this formula for success is shown by the fact

[11] *Menagiana* 1693, p. 278.
[12] *Diversités curieuses*, 1694–97, Vol. II, p. 43.
[13] *La Critique de l'Ecole des Femmes*, Scene vi.

that it was played repeatedly by Molière's troupe and later by the *Comédie-Française* throughout the century, long after the *précieuses* had ceased to be news. It was imitated by other French dramatists and translated into English (1668), German (1670) and Dutch (1685).

Such a success springs not from any reforming qualities in the play, but from its comic art as a piece of light-hearted, sparkling, fast-moving entertainment. If we still wish to do as was once customary, and look for the attitude of Molière in the words of the most reasonable character, we will not find it there. The most reasonable characters are probably La Grange and Du Croisy. It is the impostor Mascarille, however, who pronounces the final comment. When he has been ingloriously returned to his rôle of valet, he remarks: 'Je vois bien qu'on n'aime ici que la vaine apparence, et qu'on n'y considère point la vertu toute nue' but even this is a tongue-in-cheek remark, since he has just been stripped of all his finery 'jusqu'à la moindre chose'. It is not only virtue which is left quite naked on the stage. Thus even the remark which might appear to sum up whatever serious import there may be in the play is shown, by the nonsense which accompanies it, to be a joke too. Nothing is to be taken too seriously. The audience must go away laughing—and so must we.

Further Reading

On Molière

Adam, Antoine, 'La Genèse des 'Précieuses ridicules', *Revue d'histoire de la philosophie et d'histoire générale de la civilisation*, Lille, 1939, Fasc. 25, pp. 14–46.

Bray, René, *Molière homme de théâtre*, Paris, 1954

Gossman, Lionel, *Men and Masks, a Study of Molière*, Baltimore, 1963

Mongrédien, Georges, *Recueil des textes et des documents du XVIIᵉ siècle relatifs a Molière*, Paris, 1965 (*Les Précieuses ridicules*, Vol. I, pp. 111–32)

Moore, W. G., *Molière. A New Criticism*, Oxford, 1953

Mornet, Daniel, *Molière*, Paris, 1958

On Preciosity

Adam, Antoine, *Histoire de la littérature française au XVIIᵉ siècle*, Paris 1948–56, Vol. II (La Préciosité, pp. 20–46)

Bray, René, *La Préciosité et les précieux de Thibaut de Champagne à Jean Giraudoux*, Paris, 1948

Brunot, Ferdinand, *Histoire de la langue française*, Paris, 1966, Vol. III (La Préciosité, pp. 66–74; Expressions et Figures, pp. 241–61)

de Mourgues, Odette, *Metaphysical, Baroque and Précieux Poetry*, Oxford, 1953

Lathuillère, Roger, *La Préciosité, étude historique et linguistique*, Geneva, 1966, Vol. I (Molière et *Les Précieuses ridicules*, pp. 102–57). Reviewed in M.L.R. lxii/528 (1967)

Mongrédien, Georges, *Les Précieux et les Précieuses*, Paris, 1963 (anthology with introduction)